10/03

CONTENTS:

FEET
That SUCK and FEED

Diane Swanson

GREYSTONE BOOKS

DOUGLAS & MCINTYRE PUBLISHING GROUP

VANCOUVER/TORONTO/NEW YORK

Feet do more than take you from one place to another. Sometimes you use them like these kids do—just to have fun.

ALL KINDS OF FEET

There's no doubt about it: feet are neat. Some are built for special jobs, such as climbing, jumping, swimming, or racing. Others, including the pair that you own, have many different uses.

Take dog feet, for example. Paws and claws are great for running, digging, and scratching any itch they can reach. They're not good at grabbing stuff, but they can hold a bone in place for gnawing. Paws even help a dog talk. You've probably seen a pup stroke the snout of its parent or the leg of a person when it wants attention.

Small feet with sharp, curved claws make red squirrels great tree climbers. They can race up a trunk, charge along a branch, and leap to the next tree. Their front feet are also good for holding nuts and seeds while the

Big feet help keep camels from sinking into the desert sands of Africa, Asia, and Australia.

squirrels eat. And their back feet can stomp out a scolding to any animal that gets too close.

Raccoons in North and Central America have sensitive front feet with five nimble toes on each. They can pluck cherries from a tree, husk cobs of corn, crack open bird eggs, and feel for clams in muddy streams.

When raccoons make their homes in cities, their feet get them into all sorts of trouble. They unscrew lightbulbs, turn on garden taps, yank off vent screens, break through window glass, and rip off trash can lids.

spur

The male platypus (PLAT-i-pus) of Australia defends his territory with poisonous spurs on his back feet.

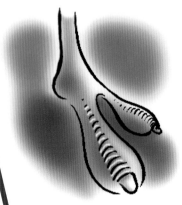

Look out for the ostrich! Its big two-toed feet can deliver a harder kick than the hooves of a horse.

Raccoon kits soon discover all the things their feet can do. These six-week-olds are using them to check out a log.

With help from its toe disks, a red-eyed tree frog in Costa Rica clings to the soft petals of a flower.

SUCKING FEET

If you had feet that sucked, think of all the things you could do: walk up walls, hang from ceilings, and even cling to glass. You could live the life of a comic book hero—or a common tree frog. Suckerlike disks on the tree frog's toes make it possible to do all these things. As well, sticky webbing between its toes helps it hold on.

Tree frogs don't spend much of their time hanging around buildings. Most kinds live in the forests of Central and South America, often high above the ground. Their toe disks help them climb and leap comfortably among the trees. They use their sucking feet to cling to branches and leaves, even to the smooth undersides.

Sea stars, or starfish, in Earth's oceans and

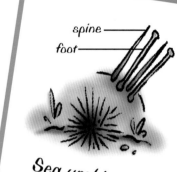

spine
foot

Sea urchins get around on tube feet with suction disks, but sometimes they walk by moving their prickly spines.

tidepools have thousands of small sucking feet. Built like tiny tubes, these feet are attached to the undersides of the animals' arms. Most sea stars have just 5 arms, but some grow 24 or more. They use the many feet on these arms to walk in any direction, but even the speediest stars take a minute to travel a meter (3 feet).

Using foot power alone, the sea stars can cling tightly to rocks and work their way straight up undersea cliffs. They can also clamp onto the double shell of a clam. Then they p-u-l-l it apart just far enough to feed on the clam's soft insides.

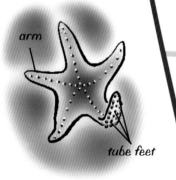

arm

tube feet

A sea star that loses an arm and its tube feet can grow a whole new set.

One foot is all a periwinkle (PAIR-i-wing-kil) has. Like a suction cup, the foot holds this little snail to rocks, wood, or grass.

Creeping, sucking tube feet made this gala gathering of sea stars possible.

Comfortably seated, the giant panda snatches more bamboo with its front paw and gets ready to eat—again.

FEEDING FEET

You can "put your foot in your mouth" by saying something you shouldn't. Other than that, it's not an easy thing for you to do. But animals such as parrots put their feet—full of food—in their mouths every day.

The giant panda of China has feet that are specially built for feeding. A long, padded bone in the wrist of each of its front paws acts like a thumb. That makes it easier for the panda to snap off a stalk of its favorite food: a thick grass called bamboo.

Before eating, the giant panda usually peels the bamboo with its front paws. Then it gobbles up as much as it can. The panda spends about 10 to 12 hours every day just stuffing itself.

It's easy for the koalas (KWAH-las) of Australia to pick and eat leaves from trees. Two toes on each of their front feet act like thumbs.

High-flying bald eagles use their feet to catch their dinners. Swooping down from the sky, they can snatch fish right from the water. The rough bottoms of their scaly feet help them hold onto slippery fish.

Each strong foot is the size of a man's hand, and each toe ends in a sharp hooked claw, called a talon. One long s-qu-e-e-ze from a foot or a blow from the talon on the eagle's back toe can kill prey such as rabbits.

Before it eats, the eagle often carries its dinner back to a tree. Its strong feet hold the food tightly while its beak tears off bits to eat or to feed to its young.

In South America, huge harpy eagles use their mighty legs and feet to yank monkeys from trees.

Crabs catch and cut food with the claws on their first pair of legs.

Clawed feet make powerful tools that help feed North America's bald eagle.

Taking a break from swimming, this river otter uses its webbed feet to hang onto a mossy log.

SWIMMING FEET

Kicking your feet helps you swim. Kicking with plastic fins on your feet helps you swim even better. Many animals have broad webbed feet—like swimming fins—that help them move easily through water. And they're not all birds such as ducks, geese, and swans. Bigger animals, including beavers and crocodiles, use webbed feet and strong tails to charge through the water.

River otters spend a lot of time in water where their webbed feet help them swim fast. Day or night, they hunt for food, chasing after fish and other small animals. Sometimes they also use their webbed front feet as shovels to dig for frogs in muddy river bottoms.

Young river otter pups are usually afraid to swim at first. They might hold onto their mother

Wide, webbed back feet power beavers as they swim. They can zip along at speeds of about 8 kilometers (5 miles) an hour.

while she swims, but in a few days, the pups learn to swim well.

Penguins can swim as soon as they hit the water. These birds are built for life at sea. Their streamlined bodies fly through water on flippers in place of wings. Their fleshy webbed feet work as rudders to help them steer. And what a great job they do! As the penguins zoom among schools of fish, they can dart easily this way and that.

In the Antarctic, penguins also "swim" across ice. Lying on their bellies, they use the claws on their feet to push off. As they slide, they shove with their feet and balance with their flippers.

With big feet paddling and wings beating, the Magellan flightless steamer duck of South America can swim more than 40 kilometers (25 miles) an hour!

Webbed toes on the back feet of sea otters in the Pacific Ocean are so long they form flippers.

Enough waddling on ice!
A penguin jumps back into
the sea, where it swims
with speed and grace.

Climbing is a cinch for a sloth. This one's just hanging loose, totally at home in a tree.

CLIMBING FEET

Climb a tree and you grip the trunk tightly. You reach for limbs and search for spots to place your toes. The climb can be tough, but it's nothing for a spider. Tufts of hair at the ends of its eight long legs make tree-climbing a breeze. Each of these hairs is split thousands of times and coated with moisture that sticks to the trunk. Spiders can even use their special feet to scamper up glass.

hooks

Little lizards called geckos can use hundreds of tiny hooks on their toes to run straight up mirrors.

In the rain forests of Central and South America, hairy sloths spend most of their time living in trees and eating leaves. Climbing is what they do best. They do it upside down as well as right side up. Using strong curved claws that are longer than your fingers, sloths swing from branch to branch on all four feet. Climbing is so natural for them they can sleep hanging upside down. They even give birth to their young high up in the trees.

Other animals are better at climbing cliffs than trees. Tiptoeing along narrow ledges, North American mountain goats scale steep rocky slopes of tall mountains. Each of their two-toed feet, or hooves, has a rubbery pad that helps the goats grip. They can leap nimbly from ledge to ledge. And if it's too narrow to turn around, the goats almost flip cartwheels to get going the right way again.

Although mountain goats sometimes slip on icy rocks, climbing helps save their lives. Predators such as wolves and bears just can't follow them up steep mountains.

The sure-footed chamois (SHAM-ee) of Europe is a champion mountain climber, leaping over rocks as tall as two doors.

Long feet and hands help spider monkeys in Central and South America climb trees fast.

Who dares to follow this mountain goat?
By grazing at the "top of the world,"
it escapes many of its predators.

A snowshoe hare leaps its way out of danger.
Even winter's snow doesn't hold it back.

LEADING FEET

Run fast, then l-e-a-p. Your feet and legs help you make a long jump. Record-making athletes can leap a distance about five times the length of their bodies. But that wouldn't impress the average grasshopper. It can jump about 20 times its body length without even taking a run at it.

Snowshoe hares of North America count on their leaping feet to save their lives. They escape predators, such as foxes, by tearing around in huge circles. With each bound, the hares cover a distance nearly as long as two beds. These hares are fast, too, racing at speeds of more than 50 kilometers (30 miles) an hour. Just to be tricky, they often jump from side to side as they go.

The big back feet of snowshoe hares gave

As it jumps onto another animal, a tiny flea often flips cartwheels in the air.

them their name. Like real snowshoes, these feet are long and wide, and they make it easy to travel across deep snow. What's more, they're always ready for action. Snowshoe hares sleep with their feet in jumping position—all set to take off.

The kangaroo of Australia uses its strong back legs and big feet as heavy-duty springs. When it leaps into action, its feet strike the ground together, driving the kangaroo ahead. It can cover the length of five beds in a single jump. About 13 kilometers (8 miles) an hour is often a kangaroo's normal traveling speed. In danger, it can go four or five times faster. Even so, a leaping kangaroo uses less energy than a racing horse.

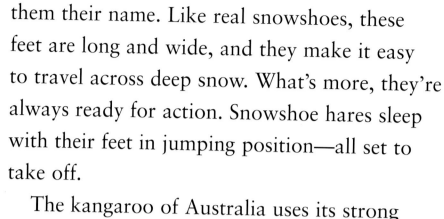

Kangaroos can jump high as well as far. They've been known to leap over fences more than 3 meters (11 feet) high.

Tree frogs can leap a distance more than 20 times their length.

Sproing! Sproing! Kangaroos make a lively picture as they bound across the desert.

It may not look graceful, but racing across water helps a swan take to the skies.

Running-on-Water Feet

You can float on water, but try to walk and you sink. You're not built like a water strider, or pond skater. That's an insect so light the surface of the water supports its weight. The hair and wax on its feet help it stay right on top.

Water striders can jump up and down on water without getting wet. But mostly they just skate around, eating smaller insects that fall within their reach. Surprisingly, a few striders have turned up on oceans, long distances from shore.

Some birds such as swans take flight from water. They manage to run on top of lakes and ponds for a few seconds. With help from their broad webbed feet and long, strong wings, they race across the surface without sinking.

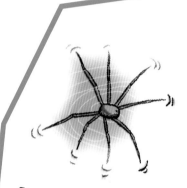

Fisher spiders sprawl across water without sinking. They jiggle the surface to attract and catch fish.

One of the world's most expert water walkers is a lizard called the basilisk (BAS-i-lisk). It lives along streams, mostly in Central America. About 80 centimeters (32 inches) long, it's no little lizard. Yet it can dash across the water to escape land-bound predators.

Running on its two back legs, the basilisk stays afloat because the water pushes up a fringe of scales on its long toes. That fringe makes its feet wider. As long as the basilisk runs fast, it can cross water without sinking. Amazingly, one basilisk was spotted racing across a lake 400 meters (440 yards) wide.

Walking on snow—frozen water droplets—is a specialty of caribou. The big feet of these northern deer act like snowshoes.

Long toes make it easy for a bird called the northern jacana (je-CAN-ah) to walk lightly across water. It uses floating plants as stepping stones.

Doing a fast dash-and-splash, the basilisk runs over water—and escapes danger.

INDEX

Greystone Books
A division of Douglas & McIntyre Ltd.
2323 Quebec Street, Ste 201
Vancouver, British Columbia
V5T 4S7

Canadian Cataloguing in Publication Data

Swanson, Diane, 1944-
    Feet that suck and feed

    (Up close)
    Includes index.
    ISBN 1-55054-767-4 (bound) – ISBN 1-55054-769-0 (pbk.)

    1. Foot–Juvenile literature. I. Cowles, Rose, 1967- II. Title. III.
Series: Up close (Vancouver, B.C.)
QL950.7.S92 2000   j573.9'98   C99-911196-5

Library of Congress Cataloguing information is available.

Packaged by House of Words for Greystone Books
Editing by Carolyn Bateman
Cover and interior design by Rose Cowles
Interior illustrations by Rose Cowles
Photo credits: Alice Thompson ii; Glen and Rebecca Grambo/First Light 3; Jim Zuckerman/First Light 4;
Jerry Kobalenko/First Light 7; Kevin Schafer/First Light 8, 16; First Light 11; Daniel J. Cox/First Light 12, 15;
Tim Christie/First Light 19; Thomas Kitchin/First Light 20; Otto Rogge/First Light 23; P. Henry/First Light 24;
John Fuller/First Light 27

Front cover photograph by Jim Brandenburg/First Light

Child models Anthony Fidler and Kimberley Cheung
through Coast Extra Events and Talent

Printed and bound in Hong Kong

The publisher gratefully acknowledges the support of the Canada Council for the Arts and of the British
Columbia Ministry of Tourism, Small Business and Culture. The publisher also acknowledges the financial
support of the Government of Canada through the Book Publishing Industry Development Program.